FIVE MAJOR ISLANDS OF THE WORLD

GEOGRAPHY BOOKS FOR KIDS 5-7

Children's Geography Books

In this book, we're going to talk about five of the major islands of the world. So, let's get right to it!

WHAT IS AN ISLAND?

One out of every six people on Earth live on an island. An island is a landmass that is surrounded by water on all sides. Continents, such as Australia, are also completely surrounded by water, but they are not considered single islands because they are so large.

Tavarua Island, Fiji

Australia

Australia is the smallest of the seven continents, but its area is more than three times as large as the area of Greenland. Greenland is the largest of all the islands on Earth in terms of landmass.

There are thousands of islands on Earth. They exist in every type of waterway—in the oceans, in lakes, and in rivers. They're also completely different from each other in terms of their size, their climate, and the types of animals and plants that live on them.

Islets in the Caribbean Sea

Many islands are really small and cover less than half an acre. These types of smaller islands are known as islets. If a smaller island is located in a river, it's known as an eyot or an ait.

A small island might just have a few rocks on its surface and little vegetation or animal life. There are also enormous islands that have thousands of square miles of land and are inhabited by millions of people.

Some islands are thousands of miles from the nearest mainland area, while others are very close and barely separated from the closest mainland. Many islands are found in groups that are closely spaced and these groups are known as **archipelagos.**

Indonesia is an Archipelago

Turbid Waters
Surround New
Zealand

TYPES OF ISLANDS

There are six major types of islands and they can be characterized by their geological structure.

CONTINENTAL

These islands were once attached to a continent and are still located sitting atop the continental shelf. They were created as Earth's continents shifted away from each other and split apart. New Zealand is an example of a continental island.

TIDAL

These islands, which are a type of continental island, can be reached by foot only when there is low tide. Sandbars or manmade structures allow travelers to get to them. However, when there's high tide, these islands are cut off from the nearby mainlands. The famous island of Mont-Saint-Michel is an example of a tidal island.

Mont-Saint-Michel, France

BARRIER

These islands, which are also a type of continental island, are aligned parallel to the coast and are narrow in shape. They can be composed of mixtures of gravel and sand and are sometimes made of coral.

They are known as barrier islands because they create a protective barrier between the mainland and the pounding storm waves of the ocean. The Outer Banks is an example of a barrier island.

OCEANIC

These islands are created from volcanoes that are erupting on the ocean floor. The layers of lava build up until they break the surface of the water. Once the top of the volcano pops out above the water, the island begins to form. The Hawaiian Islands are oceanic islands.

Island of Hawaii

Musha Cay, Bahamas, Island

CORAL

These islands are formed by thousands of small sea animals named corals. They live in colonies and they form coral reefs. Some of these reefs create thick layers that eventually break the ocean surface and create a coral island. An example of a group of coral islands, the Bahamas are located in the Caribbean Sea.

ARTIFICIAL

These islands are manmade and they are built for many different reasons. For example, in Dubai, companies are digging up sand from deep in the Persian Gulf and creating offshore islands shaped like palm trees and a world map for a real estate complex there.

Aerial View Al Marjan Island

Here are a few examples of some of the world's major islands.

GREENLAND

Greenland is a continental island and it's the largest island in the world that's not considered to be a continent. It's also North America's third largest country. It is located northeast of the country of Canada and is to the northwest of Iceland.

Frozen Greenland Fjord

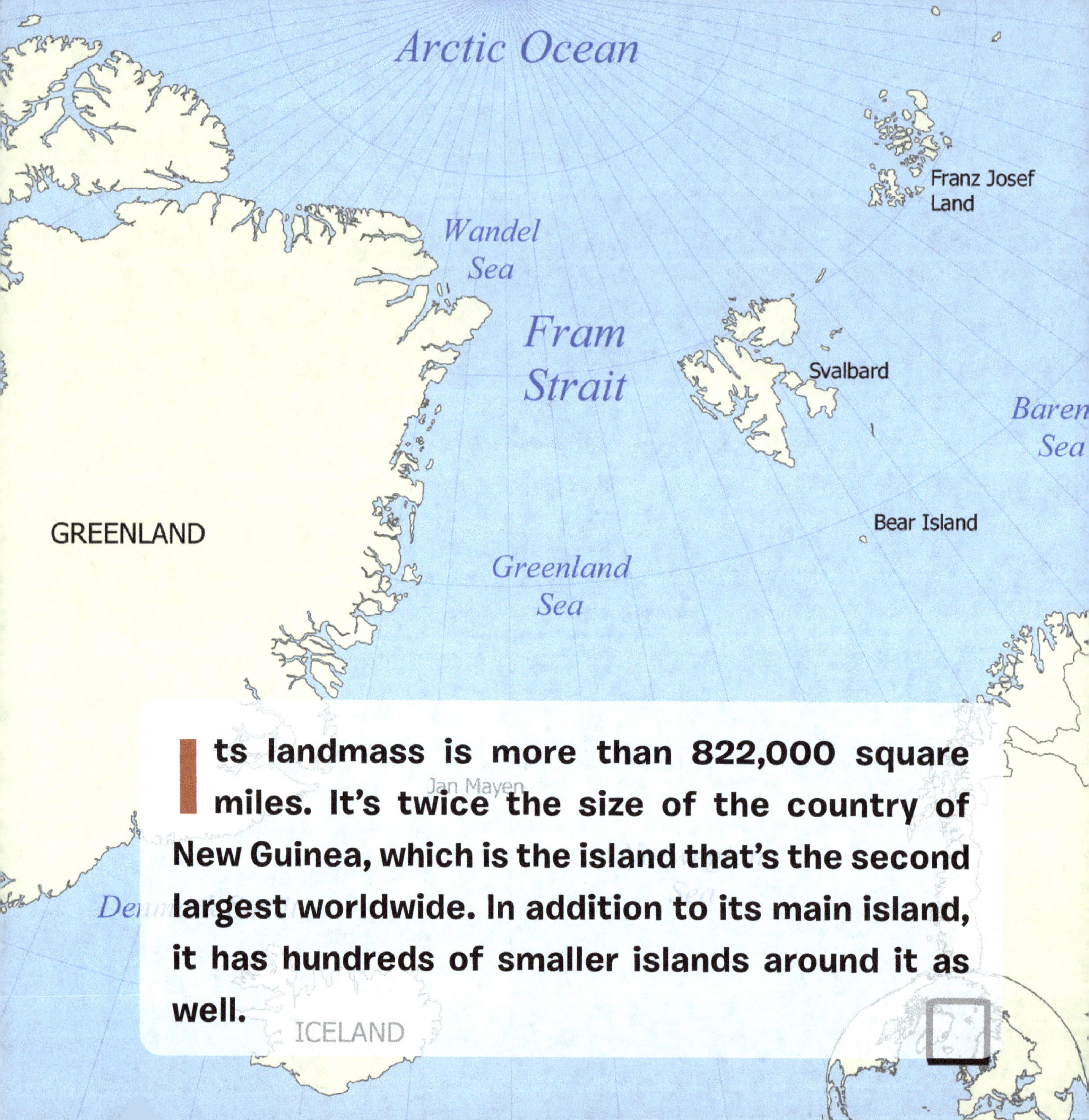

Its landmass is more than 822,000 square miles. It's twice the size of the country of New Guinea, which is the island that's the second largest worldwide. In addition to its main island, it has hundreds of smaller islands around it as well.

Greenland is misnamed because it isn't very green at all. The Vikings gave it that name to encourage settlers to come there. In fact, its surface is mostly a gigantic ice sheet that is almost 2 miles thick. Due to its climate, there are very few people living in Greenland.

The population of the entire country is about 56,000. Seventeen thousand people live in the capital city of Nuuk, which is on Greenland's west coast. Although geographically Greenland is part of the continent of North America, it's considered part of Europe since it has a political association with the country of Denmark.

Nuuk city

On Greenland the amount of ice is so enormous and so heavy that it pushes the bedrock below sea level. Also, the ice covers everything so it's only been a recent discovery that Greenland has an underwater canyon and may be three separate islands instead of just one.

Since the major portion of the island is covered by fjords, which are inlets of the sea surrounded by tall ice cliffs, no roads connect the cities. However, the people of Greenland still find ways to travel between towns by plane, helicopter, or boat. Some travel short distances by snowmobiles or sleds pulled by dogs.

Tasiilaq, Greenland

From the end of May to the end of July, the sun doesn't set in Greenland. Even during the night it glows, giving Greenland the nickname of "The land of the midnight sun." The summer month of July is the only month where the temperature moves above the level of freezing. From the middle of September through the middle of April, the beautiful Northern Lights, also called the Aurora Borealis, decorate the sky in colors.

GREAT BRITAIN

Toward the end of the last Ice Age, the islands now known as the British Isles were connected to the mainland of Europe. Their landmass extended northwest from the coasts of the Netherlands as well as the coasts of France and Belgium.

Coast of France

Scotland Crovie

The country of Scotland and a large section of Wales and Ireland were blanketed with ice as were the hills in the northern parts of what is now England.

bout 14,000 years ago, the ice began to melt and the sea levels began to rise. At that time, Ireland was separated from Great Britain and the Isle of Man was formed. As the waters continued to rise, about 2 to 4 thousand years later, Great Britain became separated from the mainland.

Southwest Isle of Man

t's thought that Great Britain became repopulated before the end of the Ice Age, prior to the time it became an island. It's also likely that Ireland was settled by sea travelers after it had become an

island. The English Channel separates Great Britain from the continent of Europe by a distance of 21 miles.

Great Britain

Great Britain is Europe's largest island as well as the largest of the islands in the British Isles. In terms of islands with the largest populations, it's ranked as third in the world with over 61 million people. It's composed of the country of England, the country of Scotland, and the country of Wales.

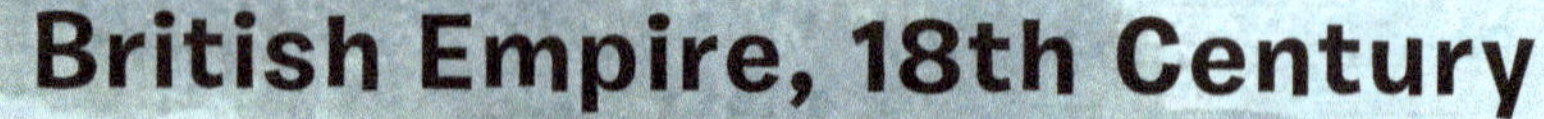
British Empire, 18th Century

In total, the island has a landmass of over 88,000 square miles, with England about 50,000 square miles, Scotland with 30,000 square miles, and Wales with 8,000 square miles. The power seat of the British Empire was located there and from the 18th century to the 20th century it was the world's largest empire and reigned over many different territories spread across the globe.

MADAGASCAR

In a ranking of islands with the largest landmass in the world, Madagascar would come in fourth. It's an island nation located off the east coast of Africa with a population of over 18 million people. As is true for many islands, Madagascar has quite a few unique animals and plants that don't exist anywhere else in the world.

Madagascar Baobab

Some of the unique animals are the giraffe weevil, named for its very long neck, the blue coua, which is a type of cuckoo bird with unique

blue feathers, and the panther chameleon, which
is one of the largest chameleons in the world at a
length of 20 inches.

Mt. Fuji

HONSHU

The country of Japan has an archipelago of over 6,800 islands, but only about four hundred of them are populated. Honshu is the largest of the islands. In addition to ranking at number 7 in a list of the world's largest islands, it is the 2nd most populated island after the island of Java. Mount Fuji, an active volcano and the highest mountain on the island, is located about 70 miles away from the island's largest city, Tokyo.

LUZON

The country of the Philippines is an archipelago with over 7,600 islands. Only about 2,000 of the islands are inhabited. Luzon, its main island, has the fifth largest island population in the world. The capital city of Manila is located there.

Manila Bay is one of the world's best harbors,
due to its location and size.

Awesome! Now you know more about five of the major islands of the world. You can find more Geography books from Baby Professor by searching the website of your favorite book retailer.

Visit

BABY PROFESSOR
EDUCATION KIDS

www.BabyProfessorBooks.com

to download Free Baby Professor eBooks
and view our catalog of new and exciting
Children's Books